NATURAL DISASTERS

BY ALLISON LASSIEUR

The Child's World®
childsworld.com

JUV NON FIC
363.34 LAS

Published by The Child's World®
1980 Lookout Drive • Mankato, MN 56003-1705
800-599-READ • www.childsworld.com

Photographs ©: iStockphoto, cover (tornado), cover
(volcano), cover (birds), 1 (tornado), 1 (volcano), 1
(birds), 4, 5, 6, 8, 8–9, 17, 18–19, 20, 24, back cover
(car), back cover (Earth); Shutterstock Images,
cover (tree), 1 (tree), 12, 13, 16–17; Mike Mareen/
iStockphoto, 2, 18; Tanguy de Saint-Cyr/Shutterstock
Images, 3, 11; Everett Historical/Shutterstock Images,
7; M. Rinandar Tasya/Shutterstock Images, 10;
Clint Spencer/iStockphoto, 14; Alonzo Adams/AP
Images, 15; JP Phillippe/Shutterstock Images, 21

ISBN 9781503844681 (Reinforced Library Binding)
ISBN 9781503846296 (Portable Document Format)
ISBN 9781503847484 (Online Multi-user eBook)
LCCN 2019957775

Printed in the United States of America

ABOUT THE AUTHOR

Allison Lassieur lived through her first tornado when she was 11 and never forgot the destruction it caused in her neighborhood. She has been fascinated by natural disasters ever since. Today, she lives and writes in upstate New York with her husband, her daughter, three dogs, and more books than she can count.

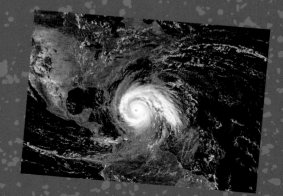

CONTENTS

Disasters happen all around the world. A disaster is an event so big and terrible that it causes massive destruction—possibly even loss of life. Some disasters come from natural forces. Tornadoes, earthquakes, hurricanes, and volcanoes are destructive natural disasters.

4

Most tornadoes happen in the Great Plains area of the United States. Hurricanes form over oceans and strike along coasts. Volcanoes and earthquakes happen along the edges of tectonic plates. These plates are sections of Earth's crust.

160 million

▲

Natural disasters affect almost 160 million people around the world every year. Despite their deadly nature, these disasters show the awesome—and sometimes strange—power of Earth. These natural events are full of odd, interesting, and just plain weird facts.

CHAPTER ONE

Shake It Up! Earthquakes and Tsunamis

Tsunami damage, Java, 2018 ▼

6

Earthquakes that happen near oceans create huge waves called **tsunamis**. In 1960, the Great Chilean Earthquake created a tsunami that traveled more than 10,000 miles (16,000 km). It hit Easter Island, Samoa, Hawai'i, Japan, and the Philippines.

An earthquake's power is measured on the moment magnitude scale. Larger earthquakes measure at higher numbers on the scale. People usually cannot feel earthquakes that measure less than a 3. The world's biggest earthquake was about 9.5 on the scale. This was the Great Chilean Earthquake in 1960.

On December 26, 2004, an earthquake shook the Indian Ocean. It caused a tsunami that struck countries in South and Southeast Asia. It killed around 230,000 people. It was the deadliest tsunami in recorded history.

The deadliest earthquake in the world hit Shaanxi, China, in 1556. This earthquake measured between an 8 and 8.3. It destroyed entire towns and killed around 830,000 people.

A 9.2 earthquake hit ▲ Alaska in 1964. It was the strongest earthquake in U.S. history. This powerhouse earthquake was so strong that the shaking even sank fishing boats in Louisiana.

Shaking and Shifting

The Great Chilean Earthquake was so strong that it sent **seismic** waves all the way around the planet. These waves shook the whole Earth for several days!

In 1811, a series of huge earthquakes struck Missouri. Waves in rivers flowed upstream. This made it look like the Mississippi River was running backward.

Parkfield, California, calls itself the "earthquake capital of the world." This tiny town has averaged one level 6 earthquake every 22 years since the 1800s.

◄ Seismographs are machines that record seismic waves.

Alaska—not California—is the state most prone to earthquakes. And it is one of the most active earthquake areas in the world. It has a level 7 earthquake almost every year! It has many earthquakes because it is on the boundary of two major tectonic plates.

In 2010, an 8.8 earthquake rocked the Chilean city of Concepción. The earthquake moved the entire city 10 feet (3 m) to the west.

Between 1975 and 1995, almost every state in the United States experienced an earthquake. The four that missed a good shake? Florida, Iowa, North Dakota, and Wisconsin.

EARTH'S TECTONIC PLATE BOUNDARIES

CHAPTER TWO

The Heat Is On: Volcanoes

10

MOUNT TAMBORA ————

The biggest volcanic **eruption** on record happened in 1815. On April 10, Mount Tambora in Indonesia exploded. That blast killed about 10,000 people. It blew enough ash and **debris** into the air to block sunlight for months.

Two years

The 1783 eruption of the Laki volcanoes in Iceland sent millions of tons of ash and gas into the air. The ash blocked sunlight and cooled Earth's climate for two years.

In 1883, the Krakatau volcano in Southeast Asia erupted. It killed more than 36,000 people and made the loudest sound ever reported in history.

One of the deadliest parts of a volcanic ▶ eruption is the pyroclastic flow. That is a fatal mixture of lava, ash, and superheated gas. A pyroclastic flow reaches up to 1,300 degrees Fahrenheit (700°C). It is so hot that it can melt metal.

Deadly Destruction

In 1980, Mount Saint Helens volcano in Washington ▶ exploded. It killed 57 people and destroyed hundreds of homes. The blast was as strong as 1,500 atomic bombs. It shot gas and rocks at more than 400 miles per hour (640 kmh).

1,500

Sylbaris's jail cell

◀ In 1902, Mount Pelée erupted. It destroyed the town of Saint-Pierre on the Caribbean island of Martinique. It killed nearly all 30,000 people in the town—except Ludger Sylbaris. He was in a partly underground jail cell. The thick walls of the cell saved him.

LAHAR FROM MOUNT AGUNG ERUPTION IN INDONESIA, 2017

Mount Pinatubo erupted in the Philippines in 1991. It unleashed volcanic mudflows, called **lahars**. A lahar is a deadly combination of water, mud, ash, and debris that flows off a volcano. The lahars from Mount Pinatubo buried hundreds of villages. It left more than 100,000 people homeless.

13

More than 23,000 people died when the Nevado del Ruiz volcano erupted in Columbia in 1985. Most of the people were killed by lahars that smashed through entire towns.

CHAPTER THREE

Twisting and Turning: Tornadoes

The wind in a tornado can reach speeds of 300 miles per hour (480 kmh). That kind of power can tear roofs off buildings, throw trains off their tracks, and toss 18-wheel trucks on their sides like toys.

One tornado was so strong that it sucked water out of the Connecticut River. It hit Springfield, Massachusetts, in June 2011.

The world's deadliest tornado on record hit Bangladesh, India. It struck on April 26, 1989. The twister killed more than 1,300 people. It also injured 12,000 more and left 80,000 people homeless.

In 2013, a monster tornado hit the area of El Reno, Oklahoma. Stretching more than 2 miles (3 km), it was the widest tornado ever recorded.

▼

Furious Wind

Tornadoes can form any time of day or night, but they are most likely to hit in the late afternoon.

A tornado hit Great Bend, Kansas, in 1915. It smashed a barn. It also supposedly picked up the five horses inside and set them down .25 miles (.4 km) away. The horses were unhurt. They were still tied together to a single post. ▶

In 2015, a tornado near Pampa, Texas, drove a cornstalk into a truck's metal radiator.

Tornadoes have hit every U.S. state. But Texas gets the grand prize for most tornadoes. The Lone Star State gets an average of 120 tornadoes every year.

In 1943, a tornado in Lansing, Michigan, pulled all the feathers off 30 chickens. The chickens survived.

A tornado hit Smithville, Mississippi, in 2011. It carried an SUV about .5 miles (.8 km). Then it smashed the SUV into a water tower.

CHAPTER FOUR

Spinning Storm: Hurricanes

The word *hurricane* comes from the Taíno people of the Caribbean. They believed in a powerful storm god called Huracán.

18

Hurricanes are large tropical storms. Their winds move in a circle and can reach speeds of 150 miles per hour (240 kmh). These storms can dump trillions of gallons of water.

In 2016, Hurricane Newton blew hundreds of seabirds all the way from the Pacific Ocean to Tucson, Arizona.

190 mph

The biggest hurricane ever recorded was Typhoon Tip in 1979. It had super strong winds of 190 miles per hour (306 kmh). The winds were so powerful that they made high-rise buildings sway.

As of 2019, Hurricane Harvey held the record for the wettest hurricane ever. It hit the Gulf Coast in 2017. That storm dumped about 33 trillion gallons (125 trillion L) of water on Texas, Louisiana, Tennessee, and Kentucky. That is enough water to fill around 50 million Olympic-sized swimming pools.

A Destructive Storm

Hurricane Katrina heavily damaged a New Orleans amusement park in 2005. The park was never rebuilt. Its ghostly remains sit abandoned outside the city.

Hurricane Katrina caused $125 billion in damage. As of 2019, that was the most of any hurricane.

The Great Galveston hurricane of 1900 goes down in history as the worst hurricane ever to hit the United States. So many people were killed that no one ever got a correct count.

Storm surges happen when hurricanes push ocean water onto land. Surges can be up to 20 feet (6 m) high and wash inland for miles. Storm surges are one of the most dangerous effects of hurricanes. Surges and flooding cause the most deaths in Atlantic hurricanes.

DANGER
BOTTOM LANDINGS SLIPPERY AND
SEA ROUGH ENTRY TO BOTTOM
LANDING IS STRICTLY PROHIBITED
BE WARNED

DANGER
BE WARNED
DEEP WATER, DANGEROUS TIDES, SEA ROUGH
AND SURFACES SLIPPERY
LEAVE IMMEDIATELY

Glossary

climate (KLY-mit) The climate is the usual weather in a certain place. Earth's climate cooled because the ash in the air blocked the sun.

debris (duh-BREE) Debris is the pieces of something that has been destroyed. The volcano threw rock debris into the air.

disasters (duh-ZASS-turz) Disasters are terrible events that cause great damage and loss of life. Disasters can be natural or human made.

eruption (i-RUHP-shun) An eruption is a sudden, violent burst of lava, steam, and rock from a volcano. A volcanic eruption can be deadly.

lahars (LAH-harz) Lahars are mudflows from a volcano that cause great destruction. Lahars contain mud, water, ash, and debris.

lava (LAH-vuh) Lava is the liquid rock that comes from a volcano. Lava can erupt from volcanoes.

pyroclastic flow (py-roh-KLA-stik FLOH) A pyroclastic flow is a destructive mix of hot ash, bits of lava, and gases that explode from an erupting volcano. A pyroclastic flow is very hot.

seismic (SYZ-mik) A seismic movement is a powerful shaking of the earth. Seismic waves can cause much damage.

tectonic plates (tek-TAH-nik PLAYTS) Tectonic plates are massive pieces of Earth's crust. Volcanoes form along the edges of tectonic plates.

tsunamis (tsoo-NAH-meez) Tsunamis are very large, deadly sea waves that are usually created by underwater volcanic eruptions or earthquakes. Tsunamis can travel many miles.

To Learn More

In the Library

Claybourne, Anna. *100 Most Destructive Natural Disasters Ever*. New York, NY: Scholastic, 2014.

Watts, Claire. *Natural Disasters*. New York, NY: DK Publishing, 2015.

Woolf, Alex. *The Science of Natural Disasters: The Devastating Truth about Volcanoes, Earthquakes, and Tsunamis*. New York, NY: Franklin Watts, 2018.

On the Web

Visit our website for links about natural disasters:

childsworld.com/links

Note to Parents, Teachers, and Librarians: We routinely verify our Web links to make sure they are safe and active sites. So encourage your readers to check them out!

Index